Sometimes I'm Afraid

by Sylvia Root Tester
illustrated by Frances Hook

THE CHILD'S WORLD

ELGIN, ILLINOIS 60120

Library of Congress Cataloging in Publication Data

Tester, Sylvia Root, 1939-
  Sometimes I'm afraid.

  SUMMARY: A young child describes some of her
fears and how she deals with them.
  [1. Fear—Fiction] I. Hook, Frances.
II. Title.
PZ7.T288So   [E]   78-23262
ISBN 0-89565-021-5

Distributed by Childrens Press, 1224 West Van Buren Street,
Chicago, Illinois 60607.

Sometimes I'm Afraid

Sometimes I'm afraid.
Once I couldn't find my mother.
I looked and looked for her.
I looked in the bedroom
and in the bathroom
and in the living room and kitchen.
I couldn't find her anywhere.
And I was scared!
I cried and cried.

But then she came up from the basement.
She had been there all along,
just doing the wash.
She hugged me and kissed me
and brushed away the tears.
And I wasn't afraid anymore.
"Next time," she said, "just call."
So now, when I can't find her,
I call. And she always answers.

We had a dog next door,
a big, big dog,
much bigger than me.
I used to be afraid of that dog.
He barked and barked.
And he was so-o-o-o big!

But one day, all of a sudden,
there he was,
standing right beside me.
And he didn't bite me!
He wagged his tail
and licked my hand. It tickled.
I laughed and laughed.
Now he's my friend.

Once there was this huge shadow on the wall,
and it raised its arms and curved them over
and shook its fingers at me.
Then it came to get me!
Oh, I was scared! I screamed!
It had me!

But it was only my brother.
He laughed, and I laughed,
and he hugged me,
and I wasn't afraid anymore.

Sometimes I have nightmares.
I wake up crying
and I am afraid,
afraid of the *meansters*
that howl in the night.

Then my daddy comes
and turns on the light
and kisses me and holds me,
holds me close.
And everything is all right.

I used to be afraid
to go on the slide.
I tried climbing that ladder,
but it was so-o-o-o high.
I looked down.
My stomach felt funny.
So I climbed down again.

But the little girl down the street
could go up fast,
and she wasn't afraid at all,
and she had so much fun!
So I took a deep breath
and I just climbed up.
I didn't look at all.
I did it! I really did it!
Now I'm not afraid anymore.

Once I ran out in the street after a ball
and a car screeched its brakes.
It almost hit me!
I was scared,
but not as scared as my mom.
She says there are some things
I ought to be afraid of.
She says I must never do that again.

I can remember,
I used to be afraid much more than I am now.
I used to be afraid of the Big Bad Wolf
in the *Three Little Pigs*.
But I'm not afraid of that anymore.
I'm bigger now.

Sometimes I'm still afraid.
But that's OK.
Everyone is afraid sometimes.

About the Artist

Frances Hook was educated at the Pennsylvania Museum School of Art in Philadelphia, Pennsylvania. She and her husband, Richard Hook, worked together as a free-lance art team for many years, until his death. Within the past 15 years, Mrs. Hook has moved more and more into the field of book illustrating.

Mrs. Hook has a unique ability for capturing the moods and emotions of children. She has this to say about her work. "Over the years, I have centered my attention on children. I've done many portraits of children. I use children in the neighborhood for my models. I never use professional models."

A great admirer of Mary Cassatt, an American Impressionist, Mrs. Hook enjoys doing fine art as well as commercial work.

About the Author

Sylvia Root Tester has been writing for children for twenty years. She has written fairy tales, folk tales, fantasy, science fiction and real-life stories, as well as supplemental teaching books. In addition, she has written works for teachers and for parents. As her own children were growing up, she tried out her stories on them. Now she uses nephews and nieces as her sounding board.

"I enjoy writing for children," she says. "If I can spark a child's imagination, or if I can make a child say, 'Yes, that's the way it is,' I've done my job."